Student Sheets

Numbered Heads

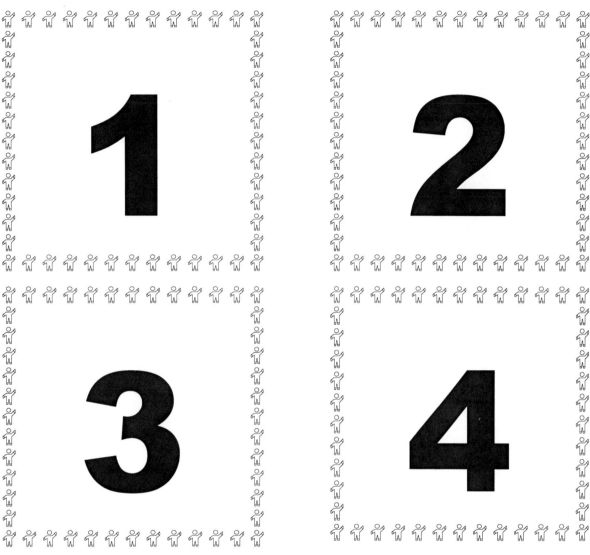

By Land or Sea?

By Land	By Sea
Theory	**Theory**
Evidence	**Evidence**

First Americans Rap

America was settled at a very early date
Ice Age hunter gatherers came across the Strait.
Cliff dwellers, totem builders, teepees in the Plains
Mound builders, longhouses, Hiawatha's brains.

Vikings heard about it when Bjarni blew off course
Leif lands in Vinland, Guitrid births Snorri.
But they didn't stay because the skraelings were sore
New faces stayed away for five hundred years more.

Henry prince of Portugal helped the captains reach
Around the coast of Africa for spices from the East.
To find a new route east, Columbus was the dude
Who sailed towards the west in fourteen ninety-two.

Portugal and Spain were the players in this game
But Johnny Cabot finally helped England stake a claim.
Balboa took his dog and marched for gold, he said.
He found the great Pacific but he lost his head.

Magellan sailed around the world, but died along the way
Enrique got there first, you know, and he was Ferdy's slave.
Epidemics, smallpox, native peoples hit the dust
As Europeans marched for gold to satisfy their lust.
To European germs, Indians had no immunity
So three out of four fell to white men's disease.

Cortés found the Aztecs and their city on a lake
Captured Moctezuma and a mighty empire quaked.
Ponce de León searched Florida for a fountain of youth
But found only poisoned arrows and death—that's the truth.

Pizarro hit the jackpot with Peruvian gold
Got rooms full of riches, made the Inca empire fold.
Estebán the African walked throughout the southern land
Sent Father Marcos crosses when he found something grand.

Coronado looked for Cíbola but landed in the dirt
Cardenas found the Canyon and Cabrillo lost his shirt.
DeSoto took his pigs and marched for four long years
He reached the Mississippi but caused many native tears.

Oñate built Santa Fe at Spain's behest
The first permanent European colony in the West.
De las Casas was a priest who sounded the alarm
Fought to keep Indians safe from Spanish harm.

The French sent Verrazano but he was no dork
He couldn't find a passage but saw water in New York
The French built a colony under Mr. Ribaut
But they nearly starved in Charlesfort, and ran back home.

The Spanish and the French made Florida a bloody scene
But the first permanent settlement was St. Augustine.
Frenchmen built Quebec, settled New France in the north,
Joliet, Marquette, and LaSalle kept exploring.

Sir Walter lost his party at a place named Roanoke
Sir Drake was a pirate and a slippery bloke.
A battle for the sea took place in fifteen eighty-eight
And the Spanish armada met a watery fate.

In one hundred years the land was explored and colonized
Rivers mapped and jungles conquered, new dreams realized.
A new nation was created when the Old World met the New;
Through natives, whites, and Africans, America grew.

Geographic Features

Directions: Label the United States Map with each landform or body of water listed below. If necessary, use an atlas to locate each one.

Atlantic Ocean
Pacific Ocean
Gulf of Mexico

Great Salt Lake
Lake Superior
Lake Huron
Lake Ontario
Lake Erie
Lake Michigan

Mississippi River
Hudson River
Ohio River
Missouri River
Platte River
Snake River
Colorado River
Columbia River

Yukon River
Arkansas River
St. Lawrence River
Rio Grande River

Rocky Mountains
Appalachian Mountains
Pacific Coast Mountains
Cascade Range
Sierra Nevada Mountains

Piedmont Plateau
Columbia Plateau
Great Basin Plateau
Colorado Plateau

Great Plains
Atlantic Coastal Plain
Gulf Coastal Plain

United States Map

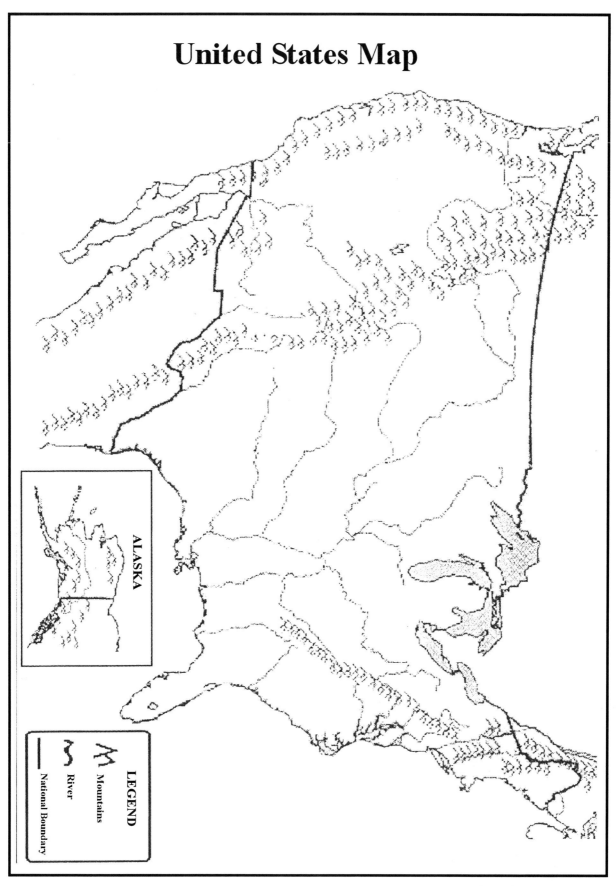

ALASKA

LEGEND

Mountains

River

National Boundary

Culture Box Evaluation

Your culture box product accurately answers your topic questions. Your illustrations show effort and creativity.	5 4 3 2 1	Excellent student product Good student product Product is correct and shows some effort Product is mostly correct but shows little effort Product is incorrect or shows little effort

Your presentation clearly and thoroughly explained your topic questions.	4 3 2 1	Excellent information Good information Adequate information Incorrect Information

Your presentation accurately presented information from several sources.	4 3 2 1	Thorough, and clear explanation Clear but no through explanation Adequate explanation Did not answer the question

Your presentation included an introduction, information connected in a clear way, and a conclusion.	2 1	Presentation organized Presentation disorganized

You spoke loudly and clearly, demonstrated good posture, and referred only occasionally to your notes.	2 1	Successful use of speaking skills Little use of speaking skills

Your presentation met the assigned time limit.	2 1	Timing correct Too long or too short

19 -18 = Excellent

17 -16 = Good

15 -14 = Satisfactory

13 -12 = Needs Improvement

11 - 6 = Unsatisfactory

Total Score _____

Your Grade _____

Indian Culture Chart

	Inuit	Anasazi	Northwest Coast	Plains	Mound Builder	Eastern Woodland	Iroquois
Food							
Clothing							
Shelter							
Customs							
Rules							
Artifacts							

How Do You Know What You Know?
Examining the Evidence

I believe the Vikings were the first Europeans to explore and settle in North America because...

Archaeology

▼ EVIDENCE

_____

_____

_____

Literature

▼ EVIDENCE

_____

_____

_____

Anthropology

▼ EVIDENCE

_____

_____

Zoology

▼ EVIDENCE

_____

_____

I Speculate that the Vikings stopped coming to America because...

▼

_____

_____

_____

_____

Spanish Exploration Wheel

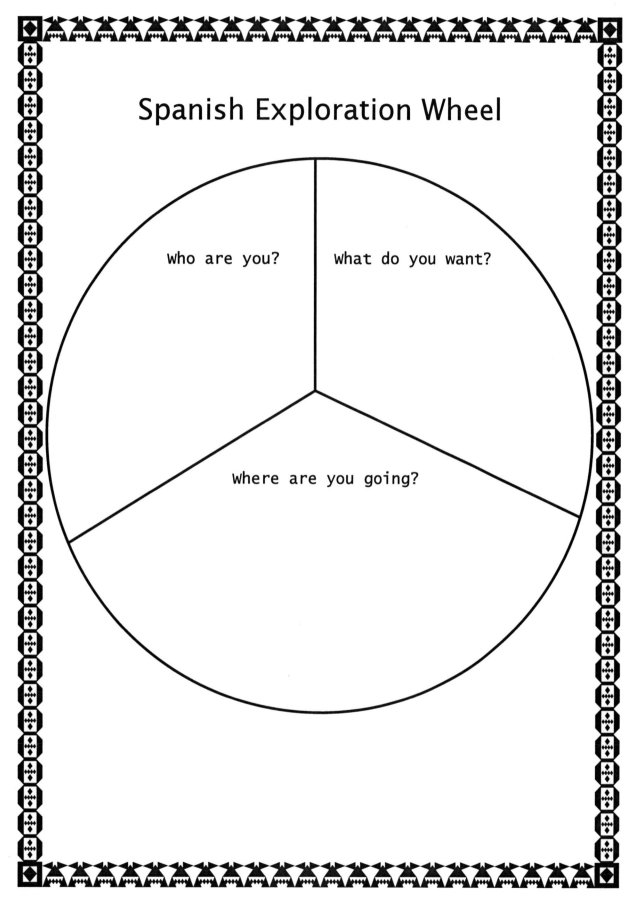

who are you?

what do you want?

where are you going?

Skit Evaluation Form

Name: _____

Spanish Explorer Profiled: _____

Your presentation accurately answered the three questions. • Who are you? • What do you want? • Where are you going?	5 Excellent student presentation 4 Good student presentation 3 Presentation is correct and shows some effort 2 Presentation is mostly correct but shows little effort 1 Presentation is incorrect or shows little effort
Your presentation was based on information from several sources.	4 Excellent information 3 Good information 2 Adequate information 1 Incorrect information
Presentation was organized and included contributions from each team member.	3 Well organized; all participated 2 Organized; most team members participated 1 Disorganized; lacking participation from several team members
In your presentation, you spoke loudly and clearly, demonstrated good posture, and referred only occasionally to your notes.	2 Successful use of speaking skills 1 Little use of speaking skills
Your presentation met the assigned time limit.	2 Timing correct 1 Too long or too short
Excellent 16—15 Good 14—13 Satisfactory 12—11 Needs Improvement 10—9 Unsatisfactory 8—5	Total Score _____ Your Grade _____

Of the Island of Hispaniola

Bartolomé de Las Casas, the first Spanish priest ordained in the New World, is known for his lifelong efforts to protect Indians from Spanish exploitation. His harsh criticism of the exploitation of natives working in the mines and the maltreatment of Indian women earned him the title "Defender of the Indians." In 1542, Las Casas denounced Spanish cruelty toward the Indians in his *Very Brief Account of the Devastation of the Indies*. That same year, Emperor Charles I prohibited the enslavement of Indians, but they continued to be exploited. Because of Las Casas' compassion for the Indians, he advised Spain to import African slaves to replace native laborers in the New World mines and fields. He later regretted his decision.

Image from an 1876 mural by Constantine Brumidi, courtesy of the Architect of the Capitol Site.

In this passage from his book, Las Casas describes the cruel ways that the Spanish conquistadors treated the inhabitants of Hispaniola, the island that now includes Haiti and the Dominican Republic.

God has created all these numberless people to be quite the simplest, without malice or duplicity, most obedient, most faithful to their natural Lords, and to the Christians, whom they serve; the most humble, most patient, most peaceful and calm, without strife nor tumults; not wrangling, nor querulous, as free from uproar, hate and desire of revenge as any in the world....

Among these gentle sheep, gifted by their Maker with the above qualities, the Spaniards entered as soon as they knew them, like wolves, tiger and lions which had been starving for many days, and since forty years they have done nothing else; nor do they afflict, torment, and destroy them with strange and new, and divers kinds of cruelty, never before seen, nor heard of, nor read of....

The Christians, with their horses and swords and lances, began to slaughter and practice strange cruelty among them. They penetrated

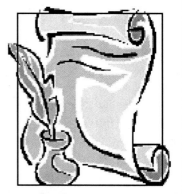

into the country and spared neither children nor the aged, nor pregnant women, nor those in child labour, all of whom they ran through the body and lacerated, as though they were assaulting so many lambs herded in their sheepfold.

They made bets as to who would slit a man in two, or cut off his head at one blow: or they opened up his bowels. They tore the babes from their mothers' breast by the feet, and dashed their heads against the rocks. Others they seized by the shoulders and threw into the rivers, laughing and joking, and when they fell into the water they exclaimed: "boil body of so and so!" They spitted the bodies of other babes, together with their mothers and all who were before them, on their swords.

They made a gallows just high enough for the feet to nearly touch the ground, and by thirteens, in honour and reverence of our Redeemer and the twelve Apostles, they put wood underneath and, with fire, they burned the Indians alive.

They wrapped the bodies of others entirely in dry straw, binding them in it and setting fire to it; and so they burned them. They cut off the hands of all they wished to take alive, made them carry them fastened on to them, and said: "Go and carry letters": that is; take the news to those who have fled to the mountains.

They generally killed the lords and nobles in the following way. They made wooden gridirons of stakes, bound them upon them, and made a slow fire beneath; thus the victims gave up the spirit by degrees, emitting cries of despair in their torture...

Reprinted by permission, Oxford University Press

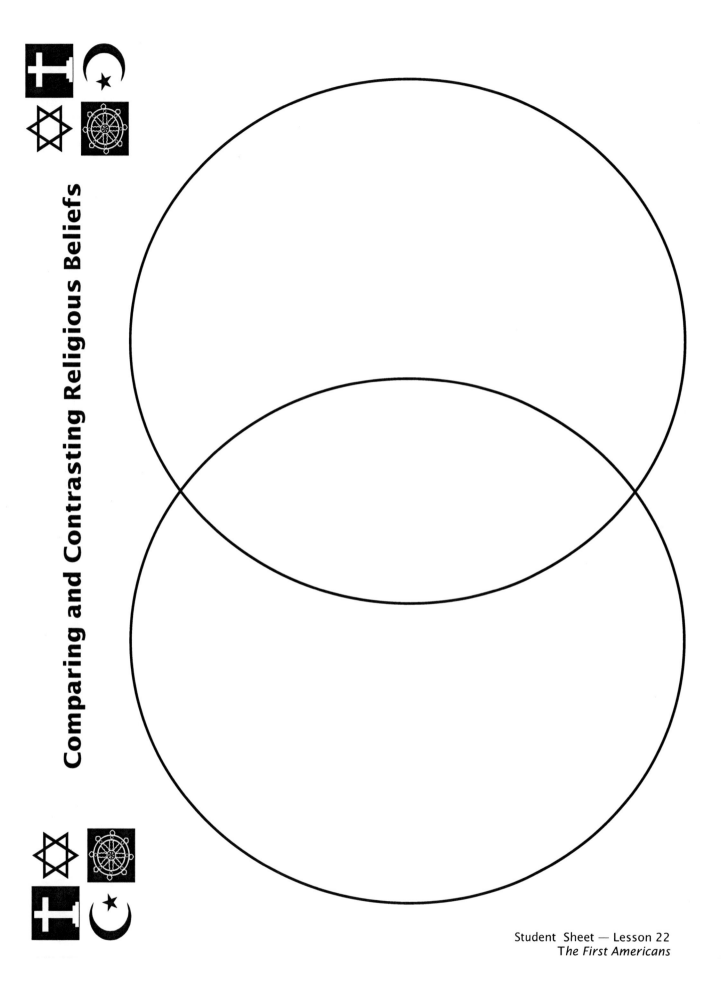

Comparing and Contrasting Religious Beliefs

Mapping the French in North America

- New France
- Champlain
- Marquette and Joliet
- La Salle
- Great Lakes
- Quebec

- Mississippi River
- Gulf of Mexico
- Louisiana Territory
- Verrazano
- Cartier
- Ribaut

- St. Augustine
- Charlesfort
- Pirates
- French Huguenots
- Fort Caroline

Team Sheets
and Document
Packets

You Can Quote Me

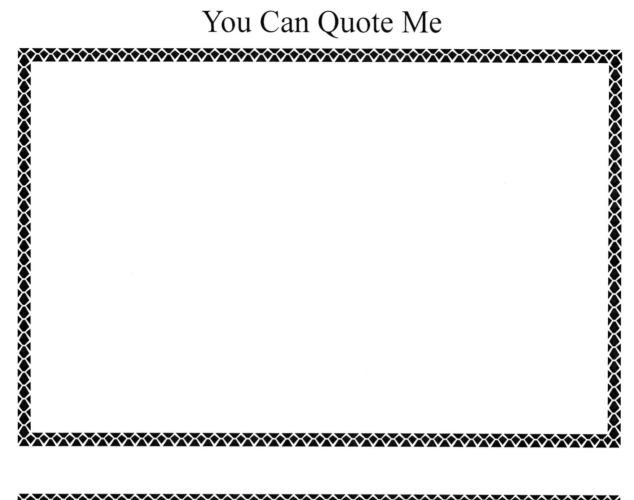

George McJunkin — Pioneer in Archaeology

In 1908, while searching for stray cattle, George McJunkin, foreman of the Crowfoot Ranch in New Mexico and a keen observer of the world around him, noticed a peculiar sight. In the far bank of a washed-out stream bed, some bleached bones glistened in the hot summer sun. McJunkin, amazed by the mammoth size of the bones, added them to the large collection of artifacts he had gathered over the years.

Born a slave, McJunkin never had any formal schooling, but to satisfy his great curiosity, he had taught himself to read. Fourteen years old when the Civil War freed him, McJunkin went west to make his fortune as a cowboy. After finding the mysterious bones, he began to spend his evenings studying maps and journals and searching in his encyclopedia, but he could not find any answers to the riddle of the bones.

Several years later, McJunkin met a young blacksmith, Carl Schwachheim, who was interested in his find. But nearly ten years passed before the blacksmith was able to visit the stream bed, and by then, George McJunkin had died. In July 1922, Schwachheim and several companions carefully excavated part of the stream bed and carried home a huge sack filled with bones. For hours, the men stared at the bones spread out on a kitchen table and pondered over the same questions as McJunkin had years ago.

In 1926, Schwachheim presented the bones to J.D. Figgens at the Colorado Museum of Natural History. The find caused a scientific sensation: they were the bones of a gigantic bison—a creature so ancient that it had been extinct for almost ten thousand years. Figgens set off to explore the bone pit and uncovered a chiseled stone spear point, embedded for thousands of years in the rib cage of the bison.

This new evidence proved that prehistoric people had hunted in North America at least 10,000 years ago. Until that find at what became known as the Folsom site, scientists believed that prehistoric bands of nomads had migrated to North America only as recently as three thousand years before.

Newspaper accounts of the dig included the story of the black cowboy, George McJunkin, who had made the original discovery almost twenty years earlier.

Adolph Bandelier — Pioneer in Archaeology

Adolph Bandelier was utterly bored. Although working in his father's prosperous bank provided an excellent income, he found the work of no interest at all. So to pass the time, Bandelier began reading science and history books, and soon became fascinated by the Spanish conquest of the Americas. He taught himself Spanish so that he could read original records of Mexican history.

Learning languages was nothing new for Bandelier. Born in Switzerland in 1840, he became fluent in his country's two neighboring languages, French and German. Educated by private tutors, young Adolph quickly added English to his collection of languages. When he was eight years old, his family moved to Illinois to found a family bank in America.

Soon Bandelier's studies and his writings about the native cultures of New Mexico were interfering with his banking duties. In 1873, Bandelier met Lewis Morgan, who later became known as the father of modern anthropology. Morgan urged Bandelier to carry out field work to learn about the native cultures and not to rely on what he read. In 1880, at age forty, Bandelier began his true life's work when he received a small stipend from the Archaeological Institute of America "to gather information on the living Indians and their history and to investigate the ruins..."

For the next ten years, Bandelier roamed over New Mexico and Arizona, investigating ruins, living with the Indians, and studying their culture. Excited about his work, the middle-aged Bandelier endured many hardships—traveling on foot through rough, unmapped desert, sleeping on the ground, and eating little. Bandelier began the practice of taking field notes of great detail about every aspect of what he saw and filled his notebooks with priceless, relevant information. Modern scholars of Pueblo Indian culture still use Bandelier's notes and research. The written history of New Mexico was five hundred years old, but its scientific history began only in 1880, when Bandelier visited the region.

Bandelier's reports and testimony of vandalism and looting of ancient Indian sites helped bring government action for their protection. In 1916, in honor of Bandelier and his work, the National Park Service established Bandelier National Monument in his favorite place among the ruins of cliff houses and dwellings of thirteenth century Pueblo Indians.

Thomas Jefferson — Pioneer in Archaeology

The man stared at the huge mound of earth. Who had built the mound? And, for what reason? Like that man, many of the early settlers were intrigued by similar mysterious mounds that dotted the landscape east of the Mississippi River. Many of the mounds were quite large (as long as a hundred feet and as high as thirty feet), and some were in the fantastic shapes of birds, snakes, and animals. The new nation of the United States was less than ten years old and American scholars were interested in the land's history before Columbus. They wanted to know, among other things, who had built the thousands of large, amazing mounds.

Although no one knew the origin or purpose of the mounds, the man staring at the monstrous pile of dirt in his own backyard decided to satisfy his intense curiosity by excavating the mound and keeping careful notes of everything he saw and did. When he carefully began to dig into that dirt, he was the first person to attempt to answer questions about the mounds through archaeology.

A marvel himself, the man was Thomas Jefferson. More often known as author of the Declaration of Independence and third president of the United States, Jefferson is also regarded as the father of American archaeology because he was the first to use modern archaeological procedures. In his mound excavation in 1784, Jefferson conducted the first systematic, well-documented archaeological dig in America. Based on his archaeological evidence, Jefferson concluded that the mounds had been constructed by the ancestors of Native Americans to bury their dead—a theory supported by subsequent archaeological findings and modern research.

Alfred Kidder — Pioneer in Archaeology

Alfred Kidder no longer wanted to become a doctor. He heartily disliked chemistry, a required course for doctors. Instead, he decided to become an anthropologist and archaeologist. Born in 1885, Kidder, a student at Harvard University, thus became only the sixth person to get his doctorate degree in archaeology.

The American southwest beckoned to archaeologists. The region's hot, dry climate preserved ancient ruins of Indian and Spanish cultures that once lived there. Kidder began his most important work at Pecos, New Mexico, at the ruins of a former Indian village called a pueblo.

Kidder made a good site choice, for Pecos had been a large Indian village inhabited for hundreds of years and a major trade center between the Plains and Pueblo Indians. In addition, the site had many undisturbed burial places. Hidden beneath the dry desert sand appeared a host of well-preserved relics, artifacts, and objects from many generations of native people who had lived, worked, traded, and died here.

At Pecos, Kidder introduced the practice of studying individual layers of a ruin. As former Pecos inhabitants put new buildings or dirt on top of locations where old things once stood, objects got buried. Because this happened many times at Pecos, older artifacts got buried deeper, with newer ones remaining closer to the surface. By studying the layers, Kidder could determine which relics were older or newer than others, and he could see how the culture of the pueblo had changed through hundreds of years.

Kidder became the first archaeologist to study the tiniest shard of everyday pottery, the bits and pieces of ancient garbage dumps, and the broken tools of ancient peoples as clues to learn how people had once lived, how tools changed with time, and even what foods people ate. Until Kidder, archaeologists collected objects for museums or private collections. Kidder felt they were only interested in "what it looks like, not what it tells."

Kidder also used new technology. In 1929, he became good friends with Charles Lindbergh, who had made the first solo flight across the Atlantic Ocean. Kidder worked with Lindbergh to locate ancient ruins using observations from airplanes.

How do we know how old is old?

Archaeologists dig up the past. They study the objects they find to reconstruct the lives of people who lived in the past. Today archaeologists use scientific techniques to examine old objects and remains. Because archaeology is the study of old or ancient things, an important part of the archaeologist's job includes figuring out the exact age of the things he or she finds.

To do this, archaeologists use two types of dating—*relative* and *absolute*.

Relative dating – In relative dating, archaeologists find an artifact to be older or newer than another, but do not know the age of either. Relative dating relies on the study of layers of materials buried in the earth. As humans put new buildings or dirt on top of locations where old things once stood, old artifacts get buried. When this happens many times, the older the artifacts are, the deeper they get buried, with the newest ones remaining closest to the surface. By studying layers of artifacts, archaeologists can often determine which are older or newer than others. Although no exact dates are determined, the archaeologist may see trends in human culture, such as how humans lived, how tools changed with time, and even what foods were eaten.

Absolute dating – In absolute dating, archaeologists use scientific techniques to figure out the specific age of an artifact. Absolute dating is done by various methods, some simple and some very complex. A method may work well on one type of material but be of no use with another. The two most important absolute dating methods are radiocarbon (carbon-14 or C-14) dating and tree ring dating. Other scientific methods include radioactive potassium dating, protein dating, and thermoluminescence.

Scientific Techniques for *Absolute dating*

Radiocarbon or carbon-14 dating — Every living thing—and anything that ever came from a living thing—contains carbon atoms. A very small amount of these carbon atoms are radioactive; these radioactive carbons are called carbon-14 or C-14, for short. Once a plant or animal dies, its carbon-14 begins to decay, slowly releasing its radioactive energy until it is all gone. It takes about 5,700 years for half the C-14 in a sample to disappear. Scientists call this its *half life.* Working in specially equipped laboratories and following carefully controlled steps, scientists measure the amount of C-14 left in the old material and compare it to the amount in the same kind of modern material. This provides an important and reliable way to tell the age of living and once-living things. However, samples older than 50,000 to 60,000 years cannot be dated because they no longer contain enough C-14 to be measured.

Tree ring dating — As a tree grows older, growth rings form in the trunk at the rate of one ring per year. When a tree grows in a changing climate, the rings differ from year to year. Wet years produce more growth and a wide ring; a dry year produces a narrow ring. When a tree is cut down, the outer most growth ring shows the last growing season or current year. Each ring closer to the core indicates one year of growth. Starting with a tree the age of which is known, such as one that has just been cut, archaeologists match and compare timbers to determine ring growth patterns. Twenty-five year overlapping patterns can accurately date back to about 9,000 years ago, but no earlier. And the method can only be used in certain areas where conditions allow wood to be preserved for a long time.

Radioactive potassium dating — Radioactive potassium dating measures the half-life of rocks in a method very similar to radioactive carbon dating. The method is used if a site is more that 35,000 years old and has no objects that were once alive.

Protein dating — The protein in bones, teeth, and other hard animal products such as eggshells breaks down at a regular rate that can be measured. One problem with this dating is that the breakdown of proteins is faster in wetter and hotter climates. Using protein decay to figure out the object's age depends on guessing the ancient temperature and climate and using only samples that contain protein and do not absorb water.

Thermoluminescence dating — When pottery, stone tools, or sand grains lie in the ground, the crystals they contain are bombarded by atomic particles (radiation) from the soil. This radiation adds energy to the atoms in the crystals, and this energy is stored in tiny flaws in the sample. Heating up the crystals makes them give up their extra energy in the form of light that can be measured in the laboratory. The amount of energy that the sample gives off when heated in the laboratory is related to the amount of time it has been in the ground since it was last fired. Only things that were once heated can be dated by this technique.

You Be The Archaeologist

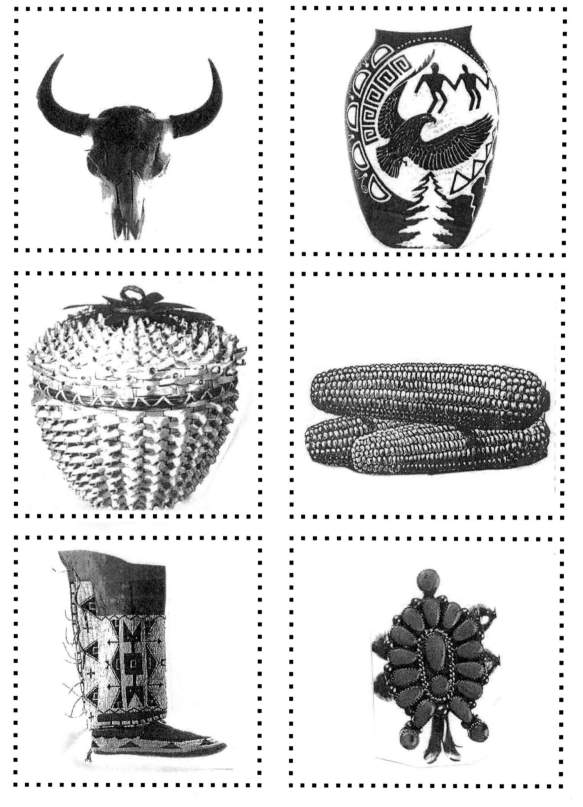

New Ways to The New World

An old Virginia sandpit may change our views of the earliest Americans

By ANDREA DORFMAN

IT IS THE AMERICAS' EPIC IMMIGRATION saga, long taught in schools and enshrined in popular books. At the end of the last Ice Age about 12,000 years ago, brave Siberians walked across the Bering Sea land bridge, then edged their way south via a newly opened corridor in the ice and fanned out in all directions. Within 500 years, their descendants had settled most of the hemisphere, from the Arctic Circle to the tip of South America. Alas, as archaeologists have learned by digging up and down the Americas, this engaging tale may be wrong.

The latest evidence against the old story was unveiled last week in Philadelphia during the annual meeting of the Society for American Archaeology. Joseph McAvoy of the Nottoway River Survey and his colleagues disclosed that an ancient campsite known as Cactus Hill, 45 miles south of Richmond, Va., has been conclusively dated at around 18,000 years old. That predates the accepted timing for the opening of that crucial ice-free corridor and bolsters the theory that the earliest Americans came by sea, possibly even from across the Atlantic rather than from Asia. "If the dates hold up, and I think they will," says archaeologist Dennis Stanford of the National Museum of Natural History in Washington, "this is probably some of the oldest material in North America, if not the entire New World."

For decades, 11,200-year-old stone spear points from a site in Clovis, N.M., have been held to be the earliest evidence of settlement in the hemisphere--and many archaeologists have been loath to give up this "Clovis first" model. But since the 1970s, it has been challenged by the discovery of still older sites on both sides of the continent, most notably a 17,000-year-old rock shelter in Meadowcroft, Pa.

Now Cactus Hill presents still more corroboration. Taking its name from the prickly pears that grow at the site, it was discovered in 1988 by a sharp-eyed farmer named Harold Conover, who alerted researchers to some curious stone tools he had spotted in road sand dug up from an old pit nearby. In 1989, McAvoy's team began excavations, now sponsored by the National Geographic Society and the state of Virginia. So far, the team has unearthed a variety of Paleo-Indian stone tools shaped for hunting, butchering and processing game; charred bones of mud turtles, white- tailed deer and other mammals;

and bits of charcoal left over from hunting parties' cooking this prey.

Radiocarbon dating and other techniques indicate the campsite was occupied as long as 5,000 years before the Clovis culture appeared. Calling the results "unequivocal," McAvoy says they should "terminate the debate over whether Clovis was first or not." The Meadowcroft rock shelter's chief investigator, archaeologist James Adovasio of Mercyhurst College in Erie, Pa., agrees. "This is another indication that people were running around North America earlier than 13,000 years ago," he says.

If so, how could they have got here? One growing possibility, long thought heretical: by boat along the eastern and western coasts of the Americas. A 12,500-year-old settlement in Monte Verde, Chile, for example, seems to have been reached most easily by water. The lack of any evidence of shipbuilding doesn't dissuade Ado Adovasio. Says he: "You had southeast Asians sailing to Australia more than 50,000 years ago."

The most startling idea is raised by Stanford, who says the Cactus Hill tools resemble even older ones found in Spain and France. He and archaeologist Bruce Bradley of Cortez, Colo., propose that the first people to reach the Americas worked their way across the Atlantic from the Iberian Peninsula some 17,000 to 18,000 years ago.

For now, few scientists are willing to go so far. "I think people did have the capacity to sail across the Atlantic," says Adovasio, "but I still think 99.9% of the peopling of the Americas occurred through the interior or along the coast from the Bering Sea." Still, he leaves a tantalizing 0.1% to begin some new mythmaking.

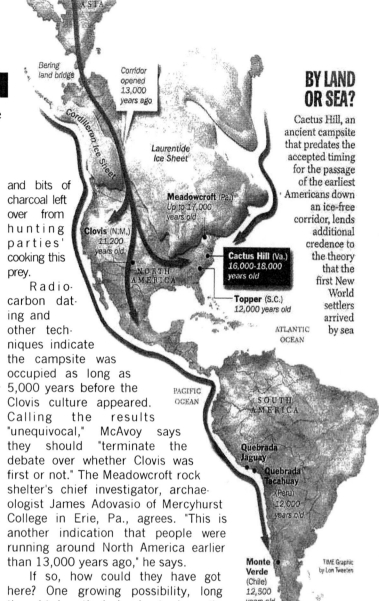

BY LAND OR SEA?

Cactus Hill, an ancient campsite that predates the accepted timing for the passage of the earliest Americans down an ice-free corridor, lends additional credence to the theory that the first New World settlers arrived by sea

Corridor opened 13,000 years ago

Bering land bridge

Cordilleran Ice Sheet

Laurentide Ice Sheet

Meadowcroft (Pa.) Up to 17,000 years old

Clovis (N.M.) 11,200 years old

NORTH AMERICA

Cactus Hill (Va.) 16,000-18,000 years old

Topper (S.C.) 12,000 years old

ATLANTIC OCEAN

PACIFIC OCEAN

SOUTH AMERICA

Quebrada Jaguay

Quebrada Tacahuay (Peru) 12,000 years old

Monte Verde (Chile) 12,500 years old

TIME Graphic by Lon Tweeten

Team Sheet — Lesson 3
The First Americans

Topic Questions

Topic 1: What did the people eat? How did the land and climate influence what the people ate?

Topic 2: What did the people wear? How did the land and climate influence the people's clothing?

Topic 3: What kind of homes did the people construct? How did the land and climate influence the people's homes?

Topic 4: What were some of the people's special customs or celebrations? How did the land and climate influence these customs?

Topic 5: What were the roles of the men, the women, and the children? How did the land and climate influence these roles?

Topic 6: What artifacts or art objects did the people create? How did the land and climate influence these artifacts?

VIKING ARTIFACTS

Picture stone found on the Swedish island of Gotland.

A Viking rune stone found in England.

VIKING ARTIFACTS

*Section from **The Saga of Erik the Red***

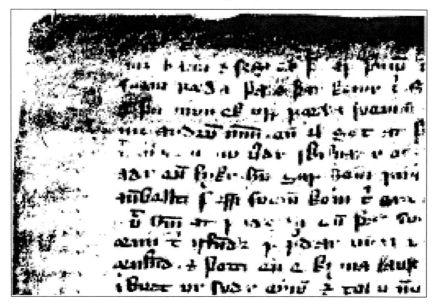

Section from the Bayeux Tapestry, an embroidered linen wall hanging made in the early Middle Ages. It shows the Norman Conquest of England, which took place in 1066. William the Conqueror, who defeated a rival king, took the throne, and created a strong central, feudal government in England—was a descendant of Norsemen from Normandy.

Note the horned figure to the top left. This is believed to represent a god or chieftain.

VIKING ARTIFACTS

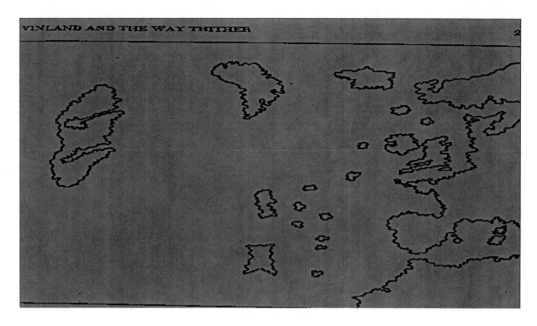

"By God's will, after a long voyage from the island of Greenland to the south toward the most distant remaining parts of the western ocean sea, sailing southward amidst the ice, the companions Bjarni and Leif Eiriksson discovered a new land, extremely fertile and even having vines, the which island they named Vinland."

Text written above the Island of Vinland from the Vinland map .

Courtesy of the Museum of National Antiquities, Stockholm

This gold and silver-plated bronze brooch was worn by a wealthy woman from Gotland, off the coast of Sweden.

VIKING ARTIFACTS

Odin's messenger, a piece of jewelry found in a grave in Uppland, Sweden

The Thor's hammer, an important Norse symbol of the struggle against chaos. According to Norse mythology, Thor used this weapon against giants and other enemies. The Thor's hammer was used in religious ceremonies.

The oldest runic alphabet, called the Futhark, dates back to 200-800 A.D. It was probably adapted from older Greek and Latin alphabets. It has no curved or bent lines because runes were meant to be carved in in trees or stones. The Futhark has 24 letters, the first of which were the letters f, u, th, a,r, and k. Runes are divided into three groups, each of which is called a "family" and belongs to a god in old Norse mythology.

Voyaging with Columbus

You are Christopher Columbus. You have just received money from King Ferdinand and Queen Isabella to finance your voyage to the Far East.

Discuss these questions with your teammates and decide what you need to know to make the voyage and what supplies you need.

- What do you need to know to make the voyage?
- What supplies will you need to take with you to make the voyage and return home?
- What criteria will you use to decide what you need to know and what supplies you need to take?
- How will you spend the money?

Remember you have to report back to King Ferdinand and Queen Isabella about the ways you used their money!

What do we need to know to make the voyage?

What supplies do we need to take with us to make the voyage?

Right or Wrong, Christopher Columbus?

Discuss the following statements that Columbus thought were true. In which cases was Columbus right?

1.   The world is not flat.

2.   Spain and Japan are on the same line of latitude.

3.   If he persisted, someone would give him money for the journey.

4.   The sea is not filled with ferocious monsters.

5.   The world is smaller than the Portuguese mathematicians thought.

6.   Nothing but ocean lies between Spain and China.

7.   China is full of splendors and riches for the taking, just as Marco Polo described it.

8.   Sailing west is the shortest route to China.

The Log of the Voyage of Columbus

 **Reader 1**

Friday, August 3, 1492

Set sail from the bar of Saltes at eight o'clock Friday and sailed with a strong sea breeze till sunset towards the south for fifteen leagues. Afterwards steered S. W. and S. by W., which is the direction of the Canaries.

Saturday, August 4, 1492

Steered S. E. by S.

Sunday, August 5, 1492

Sailed day and night more than forty leagues.

 **Reader 2**

Monday, August 6, 1492

The rudder of the caravel Pinta became unshipped making the steering most difficult. It was suspected that this had been planned by Gomez Rascon and Christopher Quintero, to whom the caravel belonged, for they dreaded to go on the voyage. The Admiral says that before setting out these men had been inclined to oppose and "pull holes," as they say. The Admiral was much disturbed at not being able to help the Pinta without danger, but he says he was somewhat quieted when he thought how brave and energetic a man was Martin Alonzo Pinzon, Captain of the Pinta. Made during the day and night twenty-nine leagues.

The Log of the Voyage of Columbus

Reader 1

Tuesday, August 7, 1492

The Pinta's rudder again broke loose. Secured it, and made for the island of Lanzarote, one of the Canaries. Sailed, day and night, twenty-five leagues.

Wednesday, August 8, 1492

There were differing opinions among the pilots of the three vessels as to their true situation, but that of the Admiral proved to be nearer the truth. He was anxious to go to Grand Canary in order to leave the caravel Pinta there, since she was steering badly and making water, and he wished to secure another vessel if one were to be found. They were unable to reach the island that day.

Reader 2

Thursday, August 9, 1492

The Admiral was not able to reach the island of Gomera till Sunday night. Because the Pinta could not be navigated, Martin Alonzo remained at Grand Canary by command of the Admiral.

Twenty-one days - August 10 — 31, 1492

The Admiral returned to Grand Canary and there with great labor and the help of Martin Alonzo and the others repaired the Pinta. Rigged her with square sails instead of the lateen sails that she had carried before. Finally sailed to Gomera.

Saturday, September 1, 1492

Saw great flames of fire burst from a high mountain on the island of Teneriffe.

The Log of the Voyage of Columbus

Reader 1

Three days -- September 2 — 4, 1492

Returned to Gomera with the Pinta repaired. The Admiral says that many honorable Spanish gentlemen, inhabitants of the island of Hierro, declared that every year they saw land to the west of the Canaries. And others, natives of Gomera, confirmed the same on oath. The Admiral here says that he remembers, while he was in Portugal in the year 1484, that a man came to the King from the island of Madeira to beg for a caravel to search out this land that was seen. This man swore that it could be seen every year and always in the same way. The Admiral also says that he remembers that the same lands of the same shape and size and in the same direction had been seen by the inhabitants of the Azores.

Reader 2

Wednesday, September 5, 1492

After taking in wood, water, meat, and other provisions which had been provided by the men left on shore when he went to Grand Canary to repair the Pinta, the Admiral was now ready to start on the long voyage with the three vessels.

Thursday, September 6, 1492

Set sail from the harbor of Gomera this morning and shaped the course for the voyage. The Admiral learned by a vessel from the island of Hierro that there were three Portuguese caravels cruising about with the object of taking him--this must have been the result of the King of Portugal's envy that Columbus should have gone to Castile to the King and Queen of Spain. It was calm the whole day and night.

The Log of the Voyage of Columbus

 **Reader 1**

Friday, September 7, 1492

In the morning were between Gomera and Teneriffe. All Friday and Saturday until three o'clock at night, becalmed.

Saturday, September 8, 1492

Three o'clock at night it began to blow from the N. E. Shaped the course to the West. Shipped much sea over the bows which made progress slow. Day and night went nine leagues.

Sunday, September 9, 1492

Sailed this day nineteen leagues, and determined to count less than the true number, that the crew might not be dismayed if the voyage should prove long. In the night sailed thirty leagues at the rate of ten miles an hour. The sailors steered badly, letting her fall away to the N. E. even to half a point; concerning this the Admiral many times rebuked them.

 **Reader 2**

Monday, September 10, 1492

This day and night sailed sixty leagues at the rate of ten miles an hour. Reckoned only forty-eight leagues, that the men might not be terrified if they should be long upon their voyage.

Tuesday, September 11, 1492

Steered a course W. and sailed above twenty leagues. Saw a large fragment of the mast of a vessel, apparently of a hundred and twenty tons, but could not pick it up. In the night sailed about twenty leagues, and reckoned only sixteen, for the reason already given.

Wednesday, September 12, 1492

This day steered the same course. Sailed day and night thirty-three leagues, and reckoned less for the same reason.

The Log of the Voyage of Columbus

Thursday, September 13, 1492

This day and night sailed W. thirty-three leagues against the currents. Reckoned three or four less. On this day, at the commencement of the night, the needles turned a half point to north-west, and in the morning they turned somewhat more north-west.

Friday, September 14, 1492

Steered this day and night W. twenty leagues; reckoned somewhat less. The crew of the Nina reported that they had seen a tern and a boatswain bird, or water-wagtail. These birds never go farther than twenty-five leagues from the land.

Saturday, September 15, 1492

Sailed day and night W. twenty-seven leagues and more. In the beginning of the night saw a marvellous bolt of fire fall from the heavens into the sea at a distance of four or five leagues.

Sunday, September 16, 1492

Sailed day and night W. thirty-nine leagues and reckoned only thirty-six. Some clouds and small rain. The Admiral says that on that day and ever afterwards they met with very temperate breezes so that there was great pleasure in enjoying the mornings. These were most delightful, wanting nothing but the melody of the nightingales. He compares the weather to that of Andalusia in April. Began to meet: with large patches of weeds, very green, which appeared to have been recently washed away from land. From this judged some island was near, though not a continent according to the opinion of the Admiral, who says, the continent we shall find further ahead.

The Log of the Voyage of Columbus

Reader 1

Monday, September 17, 1492

Steered W. and sailed, day and night, above fifty leagues; wrote down only forty-seven. Current favorable. Saw a great deal of weed which proved to be rock-weed. It came from the W. and was met with very frequently. Were of opinion that land was near. The pilots took the sun's amplitude and found that the needles declined N. W. a full quarter. The: seamen were terrified and dismayed without saying why. The Admiral discovered the cause, and ordered them to take the amplitude again the next morning, when they found that the needles were true. The cause was that the star moved from its place, while the needles remained stationary. At dawn saw many more weeds, apparently river weeds, and among them a live crab which the Admiral kept. He said that these are sure signs of land, never being met with eighty leagues out at sea. The sea-water was found to be less salt than it had been since leaving the Canaries. The breezes were always soft. All very cheerful. Strove which vessel should out sail the others and be the first to discover land. Saw many tuna fish and the crew of the Nina killed one. The Admiral here says that these signs of land came from the West, *in which direction, I trust in that high God in whose hands are all victories, we very soon shall sight land.* This morning he saw a white bird called a water-wagtail which has not the habit of sleeping on the sea.

Reader 2

Tuesday, September 18, 1492

This day and night made more than fifty-five leagues; wrote down only forty-eight. All this time the sea was very smooth and the ships sailed upon it as they would have done upon the river at Seville. This day Martin Alonzo with the Pinta; which was a swift sailer, ran ahead of the other vessels. He called to the Admiral from his caravel that he had seen great flocks of birds flying westward and that he expected to see land that night. For this reason he pressed onward. A great mass of dark, heavy clouds appeared in the north, which is a sign of being near the land.

The Log of the Voyage of Columbus

Reader 1

Wednesday, September 19, 1492

Continued on, and sailed, day and night, twenty-five leagues, experiencing a calm. Wrote down twenty-two leagues. On this day at ten o'clock a booby came to the ship, and in the afternoon another arrived. These birds do not generally venture more than twenty leagues from the land. It drizzled without wind, which is a sure sign of land. The Admiral did not wish to cause delay by beating to the windward in search of land, although he held it for certain. that there were islands to the north and south. This in fact was the case, for he was sailing in the midst of them. His wish was to sail on to the Indies, since there was such fair weather. *For if it please God,* as the Admiral says, *we shall examine these parts upon our return.* Here the pilots found their places upon the charts. The reckoning of the Nina made her 440 leagues distant from the Canaries, that of the Pinta 420, that of the Admiral 400.

Reader 2

Thursday, September 20, 1492

Steered W. by N., varying with alternate changes of wind. and calm. Made seven or eight leagues' progress. Two boobies came on board, and afterwards another, a sign of the nearness of land. Saw large quantities of weeds today, though none were seen yesterday. Caught a bird with the hand which is like a tern. It was a river bird and not a sea bird, with feet like those of a gull. At dawn three land birds came singing to the ship. They disappeared before sunset. Afterwards saw a booby coming from W. N. W. and flying to the S. W., an evidence of land to the westward. These birds sleep on shore and go to sea in the morning in search of food, never flying more than twenty leagues from land.

The Log of the Voyage of Columbus

Reader 1

Friday, September 21, 1492

Most of the day calm, afterwards a little wind. Steered the course day and night, sailing less than thirteen leagues. At dawn saw so much weed that the ocean seemed to be covered with it. The weed came from the West. Saw a booby. The sea smooth as a river, and the finest air in the world. Saw a whale, a sign of land, as they always keep near the coast.

Saturday, September 22, 1492

Steered about W. N. W., her head turning from one point to another, varying the course and making about thirty leagues. Saw few weeds. Some sandpipers were seen and another bird. The Admiral here says, *this head wind was very necessary to me, for my crew had grown much alarmed at the thought that in these seas no wind ever blew in the direction of Spain.* Part of the day saw no weeds. Later they were very thick.

Reader 2

Sunday, September 23, 1492

Sailed N. W. and N. W. by N. and at times W. Sunday nearly twenty-two leagues. Saw a turtle dove, a booby, a river bird, and other white fowl. There was a great deal of weed with crabs in it. The sea being smooth and tranquil, the sailors murmured, saying that they had got into smooth water, where the wind would never blow to carry them back to Spain. Afterwards the sea rose without wind, which astonished them. The Admiral says on this occasion, *the rising of the sea was very favorable to me, such as had only happened before in the time of the Jews when they went out of Egypt and murmured against Moses, who delivered them out of captivity.*

Monday, September 24, 1492

Continued the course W. and sailed, day and night, fourteen leagues and a half; reckoned twelve. A booby came to the ship. Saw many sandpipers.

The Log of the Voyage of Columbus

Reader 1

Tuesday, September 25, 1492

This day began with a calm and afterwards the wind rose. Continued the course W. till night. The Admiral held a conversation with Martin Alonzo Pinzon, captain of the Pinta, respecting a chart which the Admiral had sent him three days before. On this chart it appears he had marked down certain islands in the sea. Martin Alonzo said that the ships were in the position on which the islands were placed. The Admiral replied that so it appeared to him, but it might be that they had not fallen in with them owing to the currents which had always carried the ships to the N. E. and that they had not made as much progress as the pilots stated. The Admiral then asked for the chart to be returned to him, and it was sent back on a line. Then he began to plot their positions upon it in the presence of the pilot and sailors. At sunset Martin Alonzo went up on the poop of his ship and called out with great joy from his vessel to the Admiral, claiming the reward as he had sighted land.

Reader 2

Tuesday, September 25, 1492 (continued)

The Admiral says that when he heard this he fell on his knees and returned thanks to God, and Martin Alonzo with his crew repeated Gloria in *excelsis deo*, as did the crew of the Admiral. Those on board the Nina ascended the rigging, and all declared they saw land. The Admiral also thought it was land, and about twenty-five leagues distant. They remained all night repeating these affirmations, and the Admiral ordered their course to be shifted from W. to S. W. where the land appeared to lie. They sailed that day four leagues and a half W., and in the night seventeen leagues S. W.; in all twenty-one and a half. Told the crew thirteen leagues, making it a point to keep them from knowing how far they had sailed. For it was always feigned to them that all the distances were less, so that the voyage might not appear so long. Thus two reckonings were kept, the shorter being feigned and the longer being the true one. The sea very smooth. Many of the sailors went in it to bathe alongside the ships. Saw many dories, or dolphins, and other fish.

The Log of the Voyage of Columbus

Wednesday, September 26, 1492

Continued the course W. till the afternoon, then S. W. and discovered that what had been taken for land was nothing but clouds. Sailed, day and night, thirty-one leagues; reckoned to the crew twentyfour. The sea was like a river, the air sweet and very soft.

Thursday, September 27, 1492

Continued the course W. and sailed, day and night, twenty-four leagues. Reckoned to the crew twenty. Saw many dolphins and killed one. Saw a tropic bird.

Friday, September 28, 1492

Continued the course W. and sailed day and night with calms, fourteen leagues. Reckoned thirteen. Met with little weed. Caught two dolphins, the other vessels more.

Saturday, September 29, 1492

Continued the course W. and sailed twenty-four leagues; reckoned to the crew twenty-one. On account of calms made little progress this day. Saw a bird called a *Rabihorcado*, or man-of-war bird, which forces the boobies to disgorge what they have swallowed, and then eats it. This is its only way of getting food. It is a sea bird, but does not sleep on the sea and does not go more than twenty leagues from land. There are many of them in the Cape Verde Islands. Afterwards there came two boobies. The air was soft and refreshing, and the Admiral says nothing was wanting but the singing of the nightingale. The sea smooth as a river. Three times saw boobies, and a *Rabihorcado*. Many weeds appeared.

The Log of the Voyage of Columbus

Sunday, September 30, 1492

Continued W. and sailed, day and night in calms, fourteen leagues. Reckoned eleven. Four boatswain birds came to the ship, which is a very clear sign of land, for so many birds of this kind together is a sign that they are not straying or lost. Twice saw boobies. Many weeds. Note that when night falls the stars called The Guardians are near the arm on the West side, and when dawn breaks are on the line below the arm to the N. E., so that it seems in the whole night they move only three lines, which are nine hours. This is the case every night. Moreover at nightfall the needles decline a quarter N. E., and at dawn they are true with the star. From this it appears that the star moves and the needles always point true.

Monday, October 1, 1492

Continued the course W. and sailed twenty-five leagues. Reckoned to the crew twenty. There was a heavy shower. At dawn the Admiral's pilot made the distance from Hierro 5'78 leagues to the West. The short reckoning which the Admiral showed his crew gave 5 84, but the true one which the Admiral calculated and kept secret was 707.

The Log of the Voyage of Columbus

Tuesday, October 2, 1492

Continued W., day and night, thirty-nine leagues. Reckoned to the crew thirty. The sea always smooth. *Many thanks be to God,* says the Admiral here. Weeds came from the E. towards the W., contrary to their usual course. Saw many fish and took one. A white bird, which appeared to be a gull, was seen.

Wednesday, October 3, 1492

Continued the usual course, and sailed forty-seven leagues. Reckoned to the crew forty. Many sandpipers seen, and great quantities of weed, some of it old, and some very fresh, which appeared to contain fruit. Saw no other birds. The Admiral believed the islands plotted on his chart had been passed. The Admiral here says that he did not wish to keep the ships beating up and down as they had the week before, when there were so many signs of land. Though he knew there were islands in that quarter, his wish was to proceed onward to the Indies. To linger on the way he thought would not be wise.

The Log of the Voyage of Columbus

Reader 1

Thursday, October 4, 1492

Continued the course W. Sailed, day and night, sixty-three leagues and reckoned to the crew forty-six. There came to the ship more than forty sandpipers in a flock, with two boobies. A ship's boy on board the caravel hit one of them with a stone. There also came a man-of-war bird to the ship, and a white bird like a gull.

Reader 2

Friday, October 5, 1492

Continued on the course and sailed eleven miles an hour; day and night, fifty-seven leagues. Reckoned to the crew forty-five. The wind abated in the night. Fine weather and the sea smooth. *To God,* says the Admiral, *be many thanks given.* The air soft and temperate, with no weed, any sandpipers, and flying fish coming on the deck in numbers.

The Log of the Voyage of Columbus

Saturday, October 6, 1492

The Admiral continued his course and sailed forty leagues, day and night. Recoknoned to the crew thirty-three. This night Martin Alonzo Pinzon said that they had better steer from W. to S. W. The Admiral thought from this that Martin Alonzo did not wish to proceed onward to Japan. But he considered it best to keep his course, as he should probably reach thie land sooner in that direction, preferring to visit the continent first and then the islands.

Sunday, October 7, 1492

Continued W. and sailed twelve miles an hour for two hours, then eight miles an hour. Sailed, till an hour after sunrise, twenty-three leagues. Reckoned to the crew eighteen. All the vessels were striving to outsail one another and gain the reward promised by the King and Queen by first discovering land. At sunrise the caravel Nina, which kept ahead on account of her swiftness in sailing, hoisted a flag on her masthead, and fired a lombard as a signal that she had discovered land, for such was the Admiral's order. He had also ordered that at sunrise and sunset the ships should join him, as the air was more favorable at those times for seeing the greatest distance, the haze clearing away. Towards evening seeing no land, and observing large flocks of birds coming from the N. and making for the S. W., the Admiral determined to alter his course. He thought it probable that the birds were either going to the land to pass the night or abandoning the countries of the North, flying from the winter. Knowing that the Portuguese had discovered most of the islands they possessed by following the flight of birds, the Admiral shifted his course from W. to W. S. W. with a resolution to continue two days in that direction. This was done about an hour after sunset. Sailed in the night nearly five leagues, and twenty-three in the day. In all twenty-eight.

The Log of the Voyage of Columbus

Reader 1

Monday, October 8, 1492

Steered W. S. W. and sailed, day and night, eleven or twelve leagues; at times during the night, fifteen miles an hour. Found the sea like the river at Seville, *thanks to God*, says the Admiral. The air soft as that of Seville in April, and so fragrant that it is delicious to breathe it. The weeds seemed very fresh. Many land birds. Took one that was flying towards the S. W. Also terns, ducks, and a pelican were seen.

Tuesday, October 9, 1492

Sailed S. W. five leagues, when the wind changed, and then stood W. by N. four leagues. Sailed in the whole day and night twenty leagues and a half. Reckoned to the crew seventeen. All night heard birds passing.

Reader 2

Wednesday, October 10, 1492

Steered W. S. W. and sailed at times ten miles an hour, at others twelve, and at others, seven. Day and night, made fifty-nine leagues' progress. Reckoned to the crew but forty-four. Here the men could bear no more and complained of the length of the voyage. But the Admiral encouraged them in the best way he could, giving them good hope of the advantages they might gain from it. He added that however much they might complain, having come so far, he had nothing to do but go to the Indies, and he would go on until he found them, with the help of our Lord.

The Log of the Voyage of Columbus

Reader 1

Thursday, October 11, 1492

Steered W. S. W. There was a heavier sea than had been met with before in the whole voyage. Saw sandpipers and a green rush near the vessel. The crew of the Pinta saw a cane and a log. They also picked up a stick which appeared to have been carved with an iron, a piece of cane, a plant which grows on land, and a board. The crew of the Nina saw other signs of land and a stalk loaded with roseberries. Everyone breathed afresh and rejoiced at these signs. Sailed this day till sunset, twenty-seven leagues. After sunset steered their original course W. and sailed twelve miles an hour till two hours after midnight, going twenty-two leagues and a half. As the Pinta was the swiftest sailer and kept ahead of the Admiral, she discovered land and made the signals ordered by the Admiral. The land was first seen by a sailor called Rodrigo de Triana, although the Admiral at ten o'clock that evening, being on the castle of the poop, saw a light, but so small a body that he could not affirm it to be land. Calling to Pero Guderrez, gentleman of the King's bedchamber, he told him he saw light and bid him look that way, which he did and saw it.

Reader 2

The Admiral said the same to Rodrigo Sanchez of Segovia, whom the King and Queen had sent with the fleet as inspector, but he could see nothing, because he was not in a place whence anything could be seen. After the Admiral had spoken he saw the light once or twice again, appearing and disappearing like the light of a wax candle moving up and down. Few thought this an indication of land, but the Admiral held it for certain that land was near. For which reason, after they had said the Salve which the seamen are accustomed to repeat and chant after their fashion, the Admiral directed them to keep a strict watch upon the forecastle and to watch well for land. To him who should first cry out that he saw land he said he would give a silken doublet besides the reward of 20,000 maradevis a year which the King and Queen had offered. At two o'clock in the morning the land was sighted at the distance of two leagues. Shortened sail, remaining under the square-sail, and the vessels were hove to, waiting for daylight.

The Log of the Voyage of Columbus

Reader 1

Friday, October 12, 1492

When it grew light they found themselves near a small island, one of the Lucayos, called in the Indian language Guanahani. Presently they saw people, naked, and the Admiral went on shore in the armed boat, along with Martin Alonzo Pinzon, and Vincent Yanez, his brother, Captain of the Nina. The Adrniral bore the royal standard, and the two captains each carried a banner of the Green Cross, which all the ships had carried. This contained the initials of the names of the King and Queen each side of the cross, and a crown over each letter. Arrived on shore, they saw trees very green, many streams of water, and fruits of many kinds. The Admiral called to the two captains, and to others who leaped on shod:, and to Rodrigo de Escovedo, secretary of the whole fleet, and to Rodrigo Sanchez, of Segovia, to bear witness that before all others he took possession (as in fact he now did) of that island for the King and Queen, his sovereigns, making the declarations that are required, as is most largely set down in testimonies which were then made in writing. Presently large numbers of the inhabitants crowded to the shores. Here follow the actual words of the Admiral:

Reader 2

As I saw that they were very friendly to us and perceived that they could be much more easily converted to our holy faith by gentle means than by force, I presented them with some red caps, and strings of glass beads to put round their necks, and many other tries of small value, which gave them great pleasure. Wherewith they were much delighted, and this made them so much our friends that it was a marvel to see. Afterwards they came swimming to the boats, bringing parrots, balls of cotton thread, javelins, and many other things which they exchanged for articles we gave them, such as glass beads and Hawks' bells. In fine, they took all and gave what they had with good will. But they seemed on the whole to me to be a very poor people. They all go as naked as when their mothers bore them, even the women, though I saw but one girl.

The Log of the Voyage of Columbus

All whom I saw were young, not above thirty years of age, Friday well made, with fine shapes and faces. Their hair is short, Continued and coarse like that of a horse's tail. They wear the hairs brought down to the eyebrows combed towards the forehead, except a few locks behind, which they wear long and never cut. Some paint themselves black, some paint themselves white, others red, and others with such colors as they can find. Some paint the face, and some the whole body, others only around the eyes, and others the nose. They are like the Canarians, neither black nor white. Weapons they have none, nor are acquainted with them, for I showed them swords, which they grasped by the blades and cut themselves through ignorance. They have no iron, their darts being wands without iron and nothing more than sticks. Some of them have a fish's tooth at the end, others being pointed in various ways. The people are all of a good size and stature, with good faces and well made.

I saw some with scars of wounds upon their bodies, and asked by signs the cause of them. They answered me in the same way that there came people from other islands in the neighborhood with the intention of seizing them, and they defended themselves. I thought then, and still believe, that these came from the mainland to take them prisoners. It appears to me that the people are ingenious and would be good servants, and I am of opinion that they would very readily become Christians, as they appear to have no religion. They very quickly learn such words as are spoken to them. If it please our Lord, I intend at my return to carry home six of them to your Highnesses, that they may learn our language. I saw no beasts on this island of any kind, except parrots.

These are the words of the Admiral.

HERE BEGINS AN ACCOUNT OF THE FIRST TWO DAYS IN AMERICA TOGETHER WITH WOODCUTS FROM THE LETTER OF COLUMBUS PUBLISHED UPON HIS RETURN

Saturday, October 13, 1492

At daybreak great multitudes of men came to the shore, all young and of fine shapes, and very handsome. Their hair was not curly but loose and coarse like horse-hair. All have foreheads much broader than any people I had hitherto seen. Their eyes are large and very beautiful. They are not black, but the color of the inhabitants of the Canaries. Nor should anything else be expected, they being in the same latitude with the island of Hierro in the Canaries. They are straight limbed without prominent bellies, and are very well formed. They came to the ships in small canoes made of a single trunk of a tree wrought in a wonderful manner considering the country. Some of them are large enough to contain forty or forty-five men, others smaller, and some only large enough to hold one man. They rowed with an oar like a baker's shovel, and go at a marvellous rate. If they happen to upset, they all jump into the sea, and swim till they have righted their canoe and bailed it out with the calabashes that they carry with them. They came loaded with balls of cotton, parrots, javelins, and other things too numerous to mention. These they exchanged for whatever we chose to give them. I was very attentive to them, and strove to learn if they had any gold. Seeing some of them with little bits of metal hanging at their noses, I gathered from them by signs that by going southward or steering round the island in that direction, there would be found a king who possessed great cups full of gold, and in large quantities. I tried to get them to go there but found they were unacquainted with the route. I determined to stay here till the evening of the next day, and then sail for the S.E; for, according to what I could learn from them, there was land at the S. and N. W. as well as at the S. W. The natives from these lands came many times and fought with them, and proceeded on to the S. W. in search of gold and precious stones. This island is rather large and very flat, with bright green trees and a very large lake in the center without any mountain. The whole land is so green that it is a pleasure to look on. The natives are very docile, and desirous to possess anything they saw with us. But not having anything to give in return, they take what they can get and presently swim away. Still they give away all they have got for whatever may be given to them, down to broken bits of crockery and glass. I saw one give sixteen skeins of cotton thread which weighed above twenty-five pounds for three Portuguese ceutis, the skeins being as much as an arroba of cotton thread. This traffic I forbade, and suffered no one to take their cotton from them, unless I should order it to be procured for your Highnesses, if proper quantities could be met with: It grows in this island, but from my short stay here I could not satisfy myself fully concerning it. The gold, also, which they wear in their noses, is found here, but not to lose time, I am determined to see f I can find the island of Japan. Now, as it is night, all the natives have gone on shore with their canoes.

Sunday, October 14, 1492

At dawn I ordered the ship's boat and the boats of the caravel to be got ready and coasted along the island toward the N.N.E. to see the other side of it, we having landed first on the eastern side. Presently I saw two or three villages, and the people all came down to the shore, calling out to us, and giving thanks to God. Some brought us water, and others food; others seeing that I was not disposed to land, plunged into the sea and swam out to us. We understood that they asked us if we had come from heaven. One old man came on board my boat. The others, both men and women cried with loud voices, "Come and see the men who have come from heaven. Bring them food and drink." There came many of both sexes, everyone bringing something, giving thanks to God, throwing themselves on the ground, and lifting up their hands to heaven. They shouted to us to come on shore, but I was afraid to land, seeing an extensive reef of rocks which surrounds the whole island. Although within there is a depth of water and room sufficient for all the ships of Christendom, there is a very narrow entrance. There are some shoals withinside, but the sea has no more motion than the water in a well. In order to see all this I set out in the morning, for I wished to give a full account to your Highnesses, as also to find out where a fort might be built. I discovered a tongue of land which appeared like an island, though it was not one, but might be cut through and made so in two days. On it were six houses. I do not, however, see the necessity of thus fortifying the place, as the people here are simple in war-like matters, as your Highnesses will see by those seven which I caused to be taken and carried to Spain in order to learn our language, and return, unless your Highnesses should order them all to be brought to Castile, or to be kept as captives on the same island. I could conquer the whole of them with fifty men and govern them as I pleased. Near the islet I have mentioned were groves of trees, the most beautiful I have ever seen, with leaves as green as those of Castile in the month of April and May. There were also many streams. After having taken a survey of these parts, I returned to the ship, and set sail. I saw so many islands that I knew not which first to visit. Those natives whom I had taken on board informed me by signs that there were so many of them that they could not be numbered; they repeated the names of more than a hundred. I determined to steer for the largest, and so I did. It will be distant about five leagues from San Salvador; and the others, some more, and some less. All are very flat, and all are inhabited. The natives make war on each other, although these are very simple-minded and handsomely formed people.

These are the words of the Admiral

Encounter Frame

for

*Account of the First Two Days in America from the
Letter of Columbus Published Upon His Return*

Columbus

What were Columbus' **goals**?

What were Columbus' **actions**?

Tainos

What were the Tainos' **goals**?

What were the Tainos' **actions**?

How did Columbus and the Tainos Interact?

Conflict Interactions

Compromise Interactions

Cooperative Interactions

What were the **results** of the
interactions for Columbus?

What were the **results** of the
interactions for the Tainos?

Waldseemüller's 1509 Map

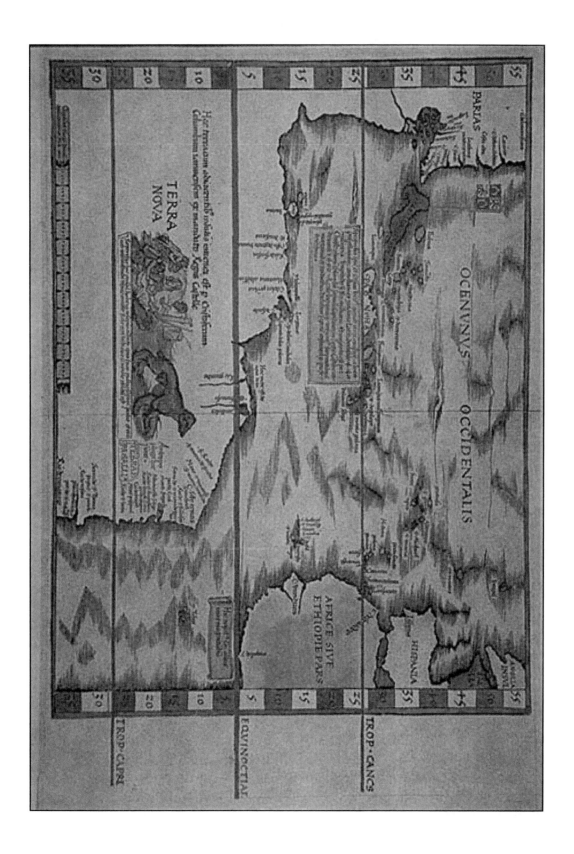

Waldseemüller's 1513 Admiral's Map

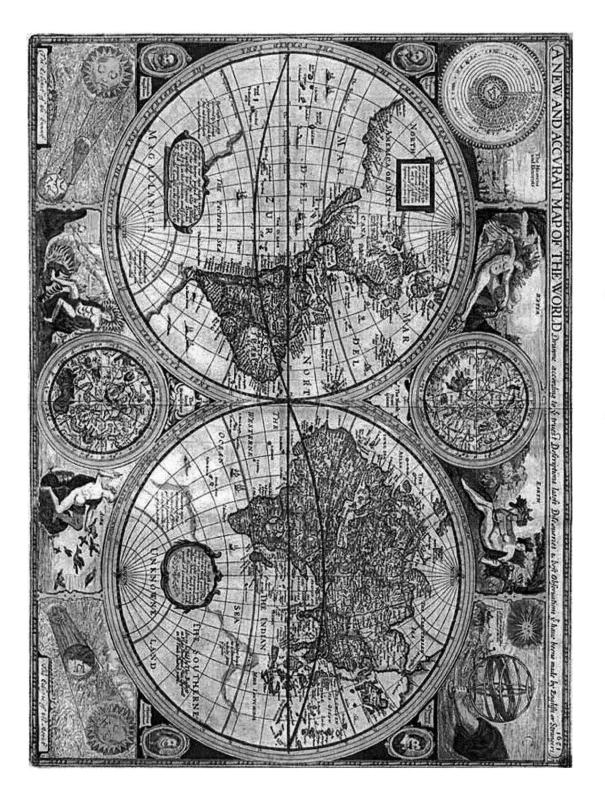

John Speed's Map of 1627

Religious Freedom in the Courts

Congress shall make no law respecting an establishment of religion or prohibiting the free exercise thereof...

First Amendment
United States Constitution

Case #1: A Life or Death Decision

In January 1990, seventeen-year-old Alexis Demos was seriously injured in a snowboarding accident. In the intensive care unit of her local hospital, doctors feared Alexis' injuries would cause her to lose a lot of blood and could even kill her. Her parents told the doctors that they—and Alexis— were Jehovah's Witnesses, and that their religion forbids blood transfusions. They believe that the Bible teaches that blood should not be transfused. Doctors, who feared that she might die if she did not receive a transfusion, asked a judge to order that Alexis be given blood in spite of her objections.

Questions to Consider
- Whose freedom of religion is at stake?
- Does an adult have the right to refuse a blood transfusion, even if this may lead to death?
- Can a parent (based on his or her own religious beliefs) refuse to allow certain medical treatments such as a transfusion to a minor child?
- What happened? How did the courts rule?

Case #2: Is Bible Club Illegal?

Bridget Mergens, a high school senior in a public high school in Omaha, Nebraska, wanted to start an after school Bible club at her school. Bridget belonged to several other clubs at school, and wanted to have the opportunity to discuss the Bible with friends after school. When she asked the school's principal for permission to meet, he refused. He believed that a voluntary Bible-discussion group could not meet on school grounds because it would violate laws forbidding the mixing of church and state. Bridget believed this was unfair, and her case, *Westside Community Schools v. Mergens*, ended up in the Supreme Court.

Questions to Consider
- Whose freedom of religion is at stake?
- Does Bridget have the right to start an after school Bible Club on school property?
- What happened? How did the courts rule?

Case #3: Is "A Moment of Silence" Constitutional?

Ishmael Jaffree's children attended a public school in Mobile, Alabama, which began each day with a "moment of silence." During this time, students were free to silently pray or meditate if they desired. Jaffree, who said he wanted his children to be "free from programmed thinking," filed a lawsuit challenging Alabama's "moment of silence" law. He felt the school was over-stepping its boundaries and encouraging the establishment of religion. A local judge ruled against Jaffree, believing the "moment of silence" was constitutional. Jaffree's case was appealed to the Supreme Court.

Questions to Consider
- Whose freedom of religion is at stake?
- Does the "moment of silence" law establish or unfairly favor religion?
- What happened? How did the courts rule?

Case #4: Should Children be Forced to Attend School?

The Amish are members of a Christian religious community who believe in separation from the modern world. Their members do not use cars, electricity, computers, or television. Many Amish believe that an eighth grade education is sufficient for their farm-based lifestyle and do not send their children to high school. They believe that forcing Amish children to attend school after age sixteen violates their religious freedom and exposes their children to influences that will damage their beliefs. Three Amish parents in Wisconsin wanted to remove their children from school after they completed eighth grade, but state law requires students to attend school until age sixteen.

Questions to Consider
- Whose freedom of religion is at stake?
- Is the state's interest in education more important than the religious rights of the Amish?
- What happened? How did the courts rule?

Religious Freedom in the Courts
Answer Sheet

Case #1: A Life or Death Decision

What happened? The judge, who did not speak to Alexis, ruled that the hospital could force Alexis to have a transfusion in order to save her life. Alexis and her parents appealed the case, and the Massachusetts Appeals Court ruled that a mature teenager could make his or her own decision on medical treatment based on religious beliefs. Alexis recovered without a transfusion.

Case #2: Is Bible Club Illegal?

What happened? The Supreme Court ruled in *Westside Community Schools v. Mergens* that the Equal Access Act did not violate the Establishment Clause of the First Amendment; students were free to form a religious club or have religious meetings on school grounds. If students are allowed to form other clubs, they cannot be denied the opportunity to have a religious club or group.

The Supreme Court's ruling upheld the Equal Access Act, which had been passed in 1984. The Equal Access Act forbade discrimination against religious speech in public schools. Congress ruled that while government cannot promote religion, it should not forbid religious speech from school grounds.

Case #3: Is "A Moment of Silence" Constitutional?

What happened? The Supreme Court ruled that Alabama's "moment of silence" law, which set aside a period for "meditation or voluntary prayer," was unconstitutional. The Court ruled that this law unfairly favored religious practice.

Case #4: Should Children be Forced to Attend School?

What happened? In the *Wisconsin v. Yoder* case, the Supreme Court held that the Amish did not have to attend school after eighth grade because the "self-sufficient agrarian lifestyle essential to their religious faith is threatened...by modern education." The Court felt that the state's concern for education was not more important than the rights of the Amish to exercise their religion.

Major Sixteenth Century European Religious Beliefs

Protestantism

God — One God, as found in the Bible, created the world and is all-knowing and all-powerful.

Man — People are created in God's image.

Sin — All people are affected by sin.

Faith — Faith in Jesus, God's Son, removes the penalty of sin. Sin is not removed by good acts, but good acts are evidence of faith.

Holy Books — The Bible is the basis for doctrine and practice.

Morality — Morality is based on the Ten Commandments and the teachings of Jesus.

Leadership — Protestants reject the belief that the pope is infallible. Every believer can understand the Bible.

Worship — Worship service centers around preaching of the Bible, with no images in worship. Place of worship is a church, chapel, or meeting house.

Afterlife — Protestants believe in heaven, hell, and a final judgment.

Roman Catholicism

God — One God, as found in the Bible, created the world and is all-knowing and all-powerful.

Man — People are created in God's image.

Sin — All people are affected by sin.

Faith — Faith in Jesus, God's Son, removes sin; grace is received through the priesthood by means of seven sacraments.

Holy Books — The Bible (with additional books, the Apocrypha included) as interpreted by the church is the basis for doctrine and practice.

Morality — Morality is based on the Ten Commandments, teachings of Jesus, and the authority of the church

Leadership — Catholics believe in the authority and infallibility of the pope and follow his teachings on matters of faith and practice.

Worship — Mass is central to Catholic life and worship. Catholics permit images in worship and believe that the Virgin Mary and saints can intercede between God and people. They worship in a cathedral, church, or chapel.

Afterlife — Catholics believe in purgatory, heaven, hell, and final judgment.

Major Sixteenth Century European Religious Beliefs

Judaism

God — One God, as revealed in the Torah, created the world and is all-knowing and all-powerful.

Man — People are created in God's image; Jews are God's chosen people.

Sin — Jews try to live the best possible life according to the Torah. They fast and pray on Yom Kippur to express sorrow for sin and receive pardon.

Faith — God made a covenant with Abraham, the ancestor of the Jews.

Holy Books — The Torah (the first five books of the Bible) and the Talmud are the basis for Jewish beliefs.

Morality — Jews follow the Ten Commandments and teachings of Moses.

Leadership — Moses was the greatest prophet and spiritual leader. Other important leaders include prophets and scholars.

Worship — Jews observe a weekly Sabbath or holy day from Friday evening to Saturday evening and other important holy days. They have no images in worship. Place of worship is a temple or synagogue where people are seated facing Jerusalem.

Afterlife — The soul is eternal.

Islam

God — One God created the world and is all-knowing and all-powerful.

Man — People are created in God's image.

Sin — All people must work to purge themselves of sin.

Faith — Faith alone is not enough; it must be joined with pure intention, and good deeds are the only way to heaven.

Holy Books — Muslims follow the Koran, which contains the teachings of Muhammed.

Morality — The five basic duties of Muslims are a verbal testimony of faith; giving to the poor; prayer five times a day facing Mecca; fasting during the month of Ramadan; and making a pilgrimage to Mecca once in a lifetime if able.

Leadership — Mohammed, God's prophet, founded Islam in the 7th century.

Worship — Muslims hold services at a mosque on midday on Friday and at other times. They allow no images in worship. They pray facing Mecca.

Afterlife — Muslims believe in a day of Judgment, heaven, and hell.

North Florida Cultures in Conflict
Native Peoples: Timucua and Seminole

Hundreds of thousands of native people lived in Florida when the first Europeans arrived in the sixteenth century. Unfortunately, warfare, dislocation, European disease, and enslavement nearly wiped out the native population.

The Timucua included at least fifteen separate tribes who shared a common language. They may have arrived in present-day north Florida 12,000 years ago. They were ruled by a great chief. French artist Jacques Le Moyne, who came to the area in 1564, created many drawings of the Timucua.

Le Moyne print: "Killing Alligators"

Originally hunters and gatherers, the Timucua gradually depended more on farming corn, beans, and squash. In the winter they moved to the forests, where they ate acorns, deer, turkeys, and fresh-water fish. One visitor described their clever method of hunting (see picture in *The First Americans*, p. 54): "They hide themselves in the skin of a very large deer. They place the animal's head upon their own head, looking through the eye holes as through a mask…. They choose the time when the animals come to drink at the river, shooting them easily with bow and arrow." They also hunted alligators.

After St. Augustine was established by the Spaniards in 1565, Spanish soldiers intermarried with native women. Because they had no immunity to European diseases, many Timucuas died from diseases such as smallpox, measles, or influenza. By 1725, only fifteen Timucua men and eight women remained. The remaining Timucuas died shortly thereafter.

The Seminoles, who lived in present-day Georgia and Alabama, moved south in the 1700s after conflict with Europeans. They helped defend Spanish mission towns, including St. Augustine, from the English. They fought three wars with the United States during the 1800s. Many Seminoles were forced to relocate to Indian Territory (Oklahoma), but some moved into the Everglades rather than leave their lands. Today, more than two thousand Seminoles live in six reservations in Florida. They call themselves "the Unconquered People."

interview questions

1. What were you doing in north Florida?
2. How did you affect other people there?
3. When did you come?
4. How long did you last? What happened to you?

North Florida Cultures in Conflict
The Spanish: A Lasting Presence

Spanish ships first landed in Florida in the early sixteenth century, nearly one hundred years before other Europeans reached the New World. Other nations wanted some of the gold that Spain continued to ship home from the Americas. Spain needed to protect its young colonies—and its shipping lanes along the coast—from other nations, pirates, and privateers.

First Muster at St. Augustine by Jackson Walker
—The Florida National Guard Heritage Art Collection

In 1565, King, Phillip II sent Pedro Menendez de Aviles with 1,500 Spaniards—including 500 soldiers—to establish forts and settlements, drive the French from eastern North America, and protect Spanish shipping routes. His group included several priests to instruct the natives in the Christian faith. He established a base at St. Augustine, considered the first permanent European colony in North America.

Menendez, the new governor of La Florida, hoped to build a Spanish empire stretching from Newfoundland to St. Augustine. The French, who wanted New World land too, had built Fort Caroline nearby. Menendez attacked the fort and massacred most of the French. He then executed French colonizer Jean Ribaut and most of his men, thus reestablishing Spanish control over Florida.

The Spanish built a series of forts from St. Augustine to present-day Charleston, but the French and the English continued to challenge Spain. The French massacred Spaniards at San Mateo (near Jacksonville) and Englishman Sir Francis Drake plundered and burned St. Augustine in 1586. The settlement survived, however, and is considered the first permanent European colony in North America. Spain lost its hold on Florida in 1763 but regained control twenty years later. In 1821, however, Spain formally gave Florida to the United States.

**interview
questions**

1. What were you doing in north Florida?
2. How did you affect other people there?
3. When did you come?
4. How long did you last? What happened to you?

North Florida Cultures in Conflict
Africans in North Florida: Free and Unfree

Spanish explorers often included free and enslaved Africans in their expeditions. The 1528 Narvaez expedition to Florida included Estebán, a black explorer who later explored the continent for six years.

Although most Africans in the New World toiled in bondage, free Africans worked as craftspeople, laborers, soldiers and merchants. Some intermarried with whites and natives, creating a new, multi-ethnic society.

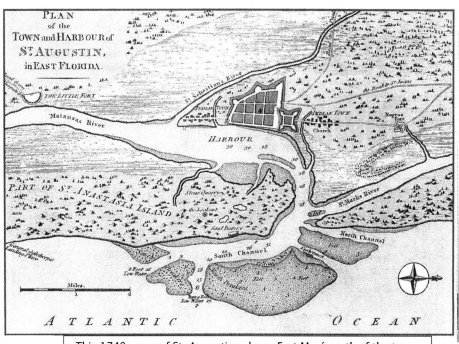

This 1740s map of St. Augustine shows Fort Mosé north of the town.

Slave rebellions took place regularly in the New World from the sixteenth century onward. Escaped Africans formed runaway communities known as cimarron or maroon towns, often forming alliances with natives. In 1686, Spaniards in Florida, hoping to disrupt English plantations to the north, promised freedom to runaway Africans who reached St. Augustine. The following year, the first recorded fugitives arrived. By 1738, more than one hundred Africans lived in St. Augustine, and they established Fort Mosé nearby. People of African descent, both free and enslaved, made up about ten percent of St. Augustine's population. When Fort Mosé was destroyed in 1740, the inhabitants moved into St. Augustine among the Spanish, Indian, and other African residents. A second fort was occupied for eleven years but abandoned in 1763 when Florida became an English colony. All the residents of the Spanish colony sailed to Cuba.

Some Africans were captured by pirates who frequently attacked ships carrying slaves between Europe, Africa, and the Caribbean. While some were forced into piracy, others chose to be pirates rather than become enslaved.

interview questions

1. What were you doing in north Florida?
2. How did you affect other people there?
3. When did you come?
4. How long did you last? What happened to you?

North Florida Cultures in Conflict
The French in North Florida: The Fort that Fell

Early three-sided fort.

In the early 1500s, France challenged Spain's claims on the Americas. King Francis I sent Giovanni da Verrazano and Jacques Cartier on several voyages to explore and search for a Northwest Passage through the continent to the Indies. Though they never found the passage, they helped France establish a claim to North America.

Jean Ribaut, a devout French Protestant, landed near St. Augustine in 1562 to establish a colony for persecuted Huguenots. He traveled north to the site of present-day Charleston and built Charlesfort. When the settlers began to run out of food and supplies, Ribaut returned to France for provisions. The thirty remaining Charlesfort colonists depended on the natives to feed them, and when the Indians refused to continue to do so, they began to starve. Desperate to escape, they built boats and attempted to sail back to France. They were rescued by a passing English ship and brought to England.

The French made another attempt at colonization in 1564, building Fort Caroline near Jacksonville. However, the Spaniard Menendez attacked the fort soon after his arrival in St. Augustine, and killed nearly all the French. Only two men escaped, one of whom was an artist named Jacques Le Moyne. He drew many pictures of life in La Florida. Jean Ribaut, who had sailed from Fort Caroline to attack the Spaniards, ran into a hurricane and was marooned off the coast. Menendez killed Ribaut and most of his men, ending France's hopes for a colony in the area.

interview questions

1. What were you doing in north Florida?
2. How did you affect other people there?
3. When did you come?
4. How long did you last? What happened to you?

A Briefe and True Report of the New Found Land of Virginia (1590)

Their manner of careynge ther Chil-   X.
dern and a tyere of the cheiffe Ladyes of the
towne of Dasamonquepeuc.

IN the towne of Dasemonquepeuc distant from Roanoac 4. or 5. milles, the woemen are attired, and pownced, in suche sorte as the woemen of Roanoac are, yet they weare noe worathes vppon their heads, nether haue they their thighes painted with small pricks. They haue a strange manner of bearing their children, and quite contrarie to ours. For our woemen carrie their children in their armes before their brests, but they taking their sonne by the right hand, bear him on their backs, holdinge the left thighe in their lefte arme after a strange, and conuesnall fashion, as in the picture is to be: seene.

B 2

The manner of makinge their boates. XII.

He manner of makinge their boates in Virginia is verye wonderfull. For wheras they want Inftruments of yron , or other like vnto ours, yet they knowe howe to make them as handfomelye , to faile with whear they lifte in their Riuers, and to fifhe with all, as ours. Firft they choofe fome longe , and thicke tree, accordinge to the bignes of the boate which they would frame, and make a fyre on the grownd abovt the Roote therof, kindlinge the fame by little , and little with drie moffe of trees, and chipps of woode that the flame fhould not mounte opp to highe , and burne to muche of the lengte of the tree· When yt is almoft burnt thorough, and readye to fall they make a new fyre, which they fuffer to burne vntill the tree fall of yt owne accord. Then burninge of the topp , and bowghs of the tree in fuche wyfe that the bodie of thefame may Retayne his iuft lengthe , they raife yt vppon potes laid ouer croffwife vppon forked pofts, at fuche a reafonable heighte as they may handfomlye worke vp-pō yt. Then take they of the barke with certayne fhells: thy referue the, innermoft parte of the lenn-ke , for the nethermoft parte of the boate. On the other fide they make a fyre accordinge to the lengthe of the bodye of the tree , fauinge at both the endes. That which they thinke is fufficientlye burned they quenche and fcrape away with fhells, and makinge a new fyre they burne yt agayne, and foe they continne fomtymes burninge and fometymes fcrapinge , vntill the boate haue fufficient bothowmes. This god indueth thife fauage people with fufficient reafon to make thinges neceffarie to ferue their turnes.

A Briefe and True Report of the New Found Land of Virginia (1590)

Their sitting at meate. XVI.

Heir manner of feeding is in this wise. They lay a matt made of bents one the grownde and sett their meate on the mids therof, and then sit downe Rownde, the men vppon one side, and the woemen on the other. Their meate is Mayz sodden, in suche sorte as I described yt in the former treatise of verye good taste, deers flesche, or of some other beaste, and fishe. They are verye sober in their eatinge, and trinkinge, and consequentlye verye longe liued because they doe not oppress nature.

C

A Briefe and True Report of the New Found Land of Virginia (1590)

A weroan or great Lorde of Virginia. III.

He Princes of Virginia are attyred in suche manner as is expressed in this figure. They weare the haire of their heades long and bynde opp the ende of thesame in a knot vnder thier eares. Yet they cutt the topp of their heades from the forehead to the nape of the necke in manner of a cokscombe, stirkinge a faier lóge pecher of some berd att the Begininge of the creste vppun their foreheads, and another short one on bothe seides about their eares. They hange at their eares ether thicke pearles, or somwhat els, as the clawe of some great birde, as cometh in to their fansye. Moreouer They ether pownes, or paynt their forehead, cheeks, chynne, bodye, armes, and leggs, yet in another sorte then the inhabitantz of Florida. They weare a chaine about their necks of pearles or beades of copper, wich they muche esteeme, and ther of wear they also braselets ohn their armes. Vnder their brests about their bellyes appeir certayne spotts, whear they vse to lett them selues bloode, when they are sicke. They hange before thé the skinne of some beaste verye feinelye dresset in suche sorte, that the tayle hangéth downe behynde. They carye a quuer made of small rushes holding their bowe readie bent in on hand, and an arrowe in the other, radie to defend themselues. In this manner they goe to warr, or tho their solemne feasts and banquetts. They take muche pleasure in huntinge of deer wher of theris great store in the contrye, for yt is fruitfull, pleasant, and full of Goodly woods. Yt hathe also store of riuers full of diuers sorts of fishe. When they go to battel they paynt their bodyes in the most terible manner that thei can deuise.

A Briefe and True Report of the New Found Land of Virginia (1590)

Passenger List
The 1587 Colonists

MEN
John White (Governor)
Roger Bailie (Assistant)
Ananias Dare (Assistant)
Christopher Cooper
  (Assistant)
Thomas Stevens
  (Assistant)
John Sampson (Assistant)
Dyonis Harvie (Assistant)
Roger Prat (Assistant)
George Howe (Assistant)
Nicholas Johnson
Thomas Warner
Anthony Cage
John Jones
John Tydway
Ambrose Viccars
Edmond English
Thomas Topan
Henry Berrye
Richard Berrye
John Spendlove
John Hemmington
Thomas Butler
Edward Powell
John Burden
James Hynde
Thomas Ellis
William Browne
Michael Myllet
Thomas Smith
Richard Kemme
Thomas Harris
Richard Taverner
John Earnest
Henry Johnson
John Starte
Richard Darige
William Lucas
Arnold Archard
John Wright
William Dutton

Morris Allen
William Waters
Richard Arthur
John Chapman
William Clement
Robert Little
Hugh Tayler
Richard Wildye
Lewes Wotton
Michael Bishop
Henry Browne
Henry Rufoote
Richard Tomkins
Henry Dorrell
Charles Florrie
Henry Mylton
Henry Payne
Thomas Harris
William Nicholes
Thomas Phevens
John Borden
Thomas Scot
William Willes
John Brooke
Cutbert White
John Bright
Clement Tayler
William Sole
John Cotsmur
Humfrey Newton
Thomas Colman
Thomas Gramme
Marke Bennet
John Gibbes
John Stilman
Robert Wilkinson
Peter Little
John Wyles
Brian Wyles
George Martyn
Hugh Pattenson
Martyn Sutton

John Farre
John Bridger
Griffen Jones
Richard Shaberdge
James Lasie
John Cheven
Thomas Hewet
William Berde

WOMEN
Elyoner Dare
Margery Harvie
Agnes Wood
Wenefrid Powell
Jane Jones
Elizabaeth Glane
Jane Pierce
Audry Tappan
Alis Chapman
Emme Merrimoth
------ Colman
Margaret Lawrence
Joan Warren
Jane Mannering
Rose Payne
Elizabeth Viccars

CHILDREN
John Sampson
Robert Ellis
Ambrose Viccars
Thamas Archard
Thomas Humfrey
Thomas Smart
George Howe
John Prat
William Wythers

BORN IN VIRGINIA
Virginia Dare
---- Harvye

THEORY
THEORY
THEORY
THEORY
THEORY
THEORY

THEORY
CARD

THEORY
THEORY
THEORY
THEORY
THEORY
THEORY

THEORY
THEORY
THEORY
THEORY
THEORY
THEORY

THEORY
CARD

THEORY
THEORY
THEORY
THEORY
THEORY
THEORY

THEORY
THEORY
THEORY
THEORY
THEORY
THEORY

THEORY
CARD

THEORY
THEORY
THEORY
THEORY
THEORY
THEORY

A report by the Archaeological Institute of America states that tree-ring data suggest that a long drought may have caused the collapse of the so-called Lost Colony of Roanoke. Studying the rings of bald cypress trees, scientists have analyzed drought conditions for the past eight hundred years. The trees show that the period during which the colony of Roanoke existed coincided with the driest spells in that area in a thousand years.

The scientists speculate that the shortage of water must have affected the colony, preventing them from producing enough food to sustain themselves. Trade with the native people would have been futile as the drought would have drastically reduced Indian food supplies also. Lack of fresh water most likely contributed to malnutrition, a leading cause of death. The settlement at Roanoke collapsed in the late 1580s with the death of all the settlers at the height of the drought.

With the establishment of the Virginia colony in 1607, Jamestown settlers carried on three active searches (two in 1608 and one in 1619) to discover what remained of the Roanoke Colony. None of the searches yielded any physical evidence of the lost colonists. However, they did find information from American Indian oral accounts, which told that colonists split into two groups, the small group went to Croatan to watch for English ships while the larger group moved to the Chesapeake Bay area. Here the Roanoke colonists lived with the Chesapeake Bay tribe for twenty years until they were massacred by Indians under the leadership of Chief Powhatan.

Accounts of Jamestown's Governor John Smith support the massacre. Smith relates a conversation he had with Powhaten in 1608: "Powhaten confessed that he had been at the murder of that colony and showed to Captain Smith a musket barrel and a bronze mortar and certain pieces of iron which had been theirs."

For years, historians believed that the colony at Roanoke failed and its colonists disappeared without a trace because they were massacred by local Indians. But the cryptic message, "Croatan" was the name of a neighboring tribe of friendly, not hostile, Indians. Some historians now maintain that instead of being massacred, the English settlement simply moved back from the coast into the swamplands where they lived with the Indians. Gradually the white colonists lost their identity as English men and women. They lived like the Indians and eventually became completely absorbed into the tribe. These historians point to later reports of gray-eyed Indians in that area. Although the stories were once considered merely legend, these historians believe they may have been true for even today gray-eyed Indians who call themselves Croatans still exist.

Maybe the first colony choose to join the Indian way of life. Perhaps, the lost colonists were simply never discovered by any future English settlers until, after generations, they were completely absorbed into the tribe.

Notable Notes About Drake

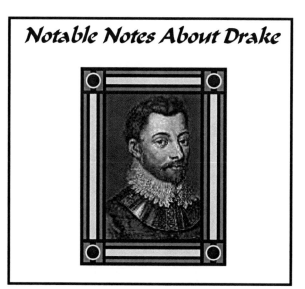

Notable Notes About Drake

Notable Notes About Drake

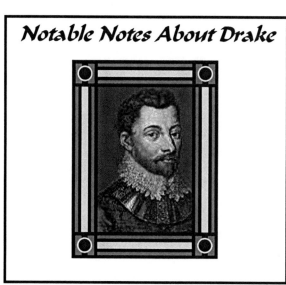

Notable Notes About Drake

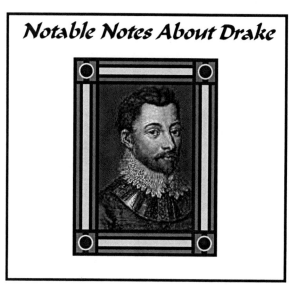

Notable Notes About Drake

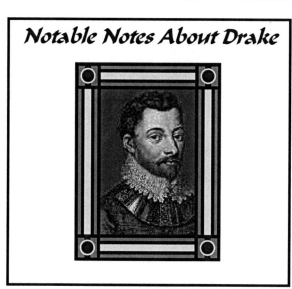

Notable Notes About Drake

Drake became known as the "pious pirate" because of his strong religious beliefs. He led religious services on board ship twice a day and preached sermons at sea to his crew.

Despite his strong religious beliefs, Drake participated fully in the West African slave trade. Drake and his relative John Hawkins made the first slaving voyages, bringing African slaves to work in the New World.

Drake considered the world and especially the riches of the Spanish as his for the taking.

Drake became a self-made man. Rising from his beginnings as the son of a poor farmer, Drake went to sea and rose to ship captain and privateer. He gained great wealth and importance, although many saw him as having risen above his station.

In Panama, cimarrones (escaped slaves who lived in the forests and mountains as outlaws) helped Drake capture treasure. One cimarrone named Diego became Drake's close friend and sailed with him around the world.

Drake gained great wealth as a privateer – a legal pirate sponsored by the English Queen Elizabeth.

Drake renamed the *Pelican* (the only ship to survive his three year circumnavigation of the world) the *Golden Hind*. Drake and the *Golden Hind* became feared world-wide.

Drake drove his men into battle by the beat of a drum that was said to have magical powers to inspire great courage.

The Spanish called Drake, *El Draque* (The Dragon) and considered him their most powerful enemy. Spanish sailors jumped into the ocean rather than face him, and Spanish mothers frightened their children into good behavior by using his name.

Drake earned the name "Master of the Sea" by learning to sail in the difficult North Sea waters. By sailing in one of the harshest stretches of water in the world, Drake learned early how to handle small vessels under arduous conditions.

On January, 28, 1596, Drake was buried at sea in the lead coffin that he carried with him in his ship's hold. Struck by a tropical disease, Drake rose from his sickbed to don his armor, so that he could die as a soldier. Drake, in his coffin, still rests on the bottom of the ocean a few miles from the entrance of the Panama Canal.

Drake went to sea at age ten as apprentice to an elderly master of a small coastal freighter. When the old captain died he willed the ship to Drake.

One of Drake's legends tells ofa magic mirror that showed him the location of every ship on the high seas.

Because Drake robbed Spanish ports and ships of so much treasure, King Philip of Spain demanded that Drake's head be brought to him on a platter.

Drake with five ships and 164 seamen started on a raid of Spanish ships and ports but ended with a voyage around the world that took three years. Only one ship, the *Pelican*, and fifty-eight sailors returned.

Drake first commanded a ship at age sixteen when he became master of a ship willed to him by an old sea captain.

As a young boy, Drake and his family lived near the sea in the hulk of an old ship.

Drake became known as a buccaneer prince. Drake was kind to his captives, but beheaded his best friend upon learning he had conspired against him.

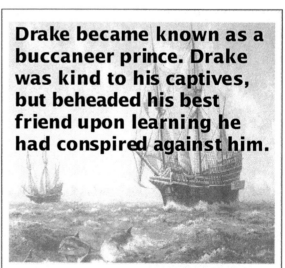

Drake studied naval warfare and made many innovations such as using rowboats to quickly turn ships to fire or avoid cannons. As commander of the English navy, he refitted ships to be speedier.

Drake was the first Englishman to sail the Pacific Ocean and to circumnavigate the globe.

Returning from a raid on the Spaniards in 1586, Drake brought the despairing Roanoke colonists back home to England.

Drake claimed the western coast of North American (present-day California) for Queen Elizabeth and named it *Nova Albion* (New England).

Drake raided Spanish supplies before the Armada sailed leaving the Spanish short of some provisions Because Drake had destroyed the seasoned wood for water barrels, the Spanish had to use unseasoned wood which rotted and made the water undrinkable. Drake called the raid "the singeing of the King of Spain's beard."

Drake was married twice. First to Mary Newman who died leaving Drake (who had just been knighted) a widower. Four years later, Drake, now rich and famous, married Elizabeth Sydenham, who was twenty years younger and came from a wealthy and important family. Drake had no children with either wife.

LaVergne, TN USA
28 April 2010
180778LV00001B/9/P